1/08

LAND ABUSE AND SOIL EROSION

UNDERSTANDING GLOBAL ISSUES

Published by Weigl Publishers Inc.
350 5th Avenue, Suite 3304, PMB 6G
New York, NY 10118-0069 USA
www.weigl.com

This book is based on *Losing the Earth: Land Abuse and Soil Erosion*
Copyright ©2002 Understanding Global Issues Ltd., Cheltenham, England

Library of Congress Cataloging-in-Publication Data

Redlin, Janice L., editor
  Land abuse and soil erosion / Janice L. Redlin.
    p. cm. -- (Understanding global issues)
  Includes bibliographical references and index.
  ISBN 1-59036-237-3 (library binding : alk. paper) -- ISBN 1-59036-511-9 (soft cover :
alk. paper)
  1. Soils--Juvenile literature. 2. Soils--Environmental aspects--Juvenile literature. 3. Soil
erosion--Juvenile literature. 4. Land degradation--Juvenile literature. I. Title. II. Series.
  S591.3.R44 2005
  333.73'137--dc22

                              2004007077

              Printed in the United States of America
              1 2 3 4 5 6 7 8 9 0 10 09 08 07 06

EDITOR Janice L. Redlin **DESIGNER** Terry Paulhus

Contents

Conservation of the planet's soil as a healthy and productive resource is vital. All terrestrial life depends on the soil, and 90 percent of food production derives from land-based agriculture. The reality is that soil is being lost or **contaminated** on a vast scale.

The extent of **degradation** is hard to measure. Some estimates appear to have been exaggerated. A recent study by the United Nations (UN), titled the Global Assessment of Soil Degradation (GLASOD), estimated that 38 percent of the world's cropland was degraded between 1945 and 1990 (74 percent in Central America). Experts working at the European Forum on Agricultural Research for Development (EFARD) reported in May 2002 that two-thirds of agricultural land had been affected by soil degradation over the past 50 years. Problems include **erosion**, **salinization**, waterlogging, weed infestation, compaction, **acidification**, **desertification**, and loss of soil fertility. Human-induced desertification, such as the degradation of soil in dryland areas, is a problem that affects 70 percent of agricultural land in arid areas of the world and is closely linked to poverty.

With the world's population already more than 6 billion and increasing at 76 million a year, the capacity of the soil to produce enough food is being stretched to the limit in some regions. While China has increased per capita cereal production by 48 percent since 1970, cereal production in Africa has fallen by 9 percent.

It is not just the developing countries that are experiencing damage to the soil. The Natural Resources Conservation Service

---

Agriculture has become agribusiness, and the care of the land often comes a poor second to maximizing output.

---

has estimated that about 1.3 billion tons (1.2 billion tons) of soil are being lost from cropland in the United States each year. Much of the topsoil has suffered from a gradual loss of organic carbon, including a reduction in soil biodiversity. Millions of acres are contaminated with industrial and urban waste.

Farmers have cultivated crops for the marketplace for many years. However, with new technology, improved methods, and shifting consumer demands, the marketplace has undergone enormous change. Agriculture has become agribusiness, and the care of the land often comes a poor second to maximizing output. Factory farming has appeared to be much more profitable than it really is by ignoring the capital expense of soil degradation and other environmental costs. The problems vary from place to place, but reach all parts of the globe. In many hilly areas of the developing world, deforestation on steep slopes has resulted in landslides and loss of soil into the rivers. Traditional practices, such as slash and burn and shifted cultivation—**sustainable** on a small scale—often leave a trail of damage that leads to serious erosion when practiced by large numbers of people. Even irrigation can destroy the soil by bringing salts or acids to the surface.

The problem of soil degradation cannot be solved quickly or easily. An essential part of that challenge is understanding the key role that soil plays in human survival.

■ **Some vineyards use organic pest-control methods, such as compost.**

Soil—The Life Giver

The thin crust of soil that covers Earth's surface carries in its apparently inert mass the foundation of all terrestrial life. Without soil there could be no plants or animals. Without plants and animals, humans could not survive. Thus, conservation of the soil is essential for human survival.

Soil is a complex material made up of particles derived from rocks, minerals, decaying organisms, living organisms, water, and gases. This complexity is easily disrupted by insensitive tillage or by inputs such as **toxic** chemicals that disturb the balance of the soil.

Soil is not a finite resource that can never be renewed. New soil is being created continuously by the action of the climate on rock and the chemical processes of decay. It takes 3,000–12,000 years to create a layer of soil sufficient to support agriculture.

Without soil there could be no plants and therefore no animals.

Obviously, people cannot afford to wait for nature to replace the soil that has been lost, and humans are unable to manufacture artificial soil that matches the quality of the natural product. Even if this could be done, it would not be feasible to deliver it to those places where it is most needed. The only realistic course is to conserve what is still available.

Life is sustained by soil and returns to it in a continuous process of recycling. Most plants depend on the soil for their nutrients. As they grow

Corn is a soil-building crop that protects soil from erosion.

and mature, the leaves they shed add to the soil's richness. All animals are absorbed by the soil in one way or another—through the droppings of the predators who eat them, through their own droppings and, finally, through decomposition. Except for material dumped in the sea and the few objects that are abandoned in space, all living and inanimate things fall into the soil.

The process of absorption also applies to materials that damage rather than enhance the soil. Thus, all pollution eventually finds its way into the ground. The waste created by modern society is routinely buried in the ground.

In the United States, about 154 million tons (140 million t) of municipal waste is buried in landfill sites each year. Much of this is inorganic material that will not easily rot or that may leave toxic chemicals in the soil. Many landfill sites are not properly sealed, and

GEOLOGY OF SOIL

The soil lies at the heart of a system that connects human life with the geological forces that shape the physical world. Earth's crust has movements that thrust rocks to the surface, where the processes of weathering and chemical reaction eventually break down the rock into tiny fragments. Climate, vegetation, and the animal world interact with this material to create the fertile soil that supports most forms of life.

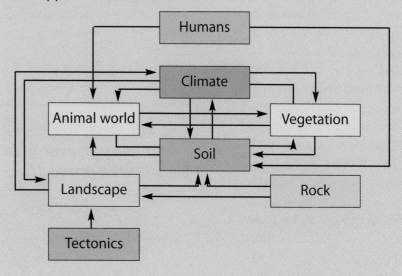

contamination can reach groundwater systems.

Acid rain, on the other hand, falls over large areas of the planet. It, too, affects the character and performance of the soil, by killing trees and by affecting the chemistry of the clay/**humus** mixture that gives soil its fertility.

KEY CONCEPTS

Acid rain Acid rain is snow, ice, or fog that is polluted by acid in the atmosphere and damages the environment. The two common air pollutants that acidify rain are sulfur dioxide and nitrogen oxide. When the environment cannot neutralize the acid being deposited, damage occurs. This can affect soil fertility, and cause extensive damage to wildlife, forests, and buildings.

Tillage Deep plowing both disrupts soil structure and leaves loose material on the surface where it can easily be eroded. Many farmers employ methods such as ridge tillage (in which only the tops of ridges are tilled for planting), chisel plowing (which does not turn the soil upside down), shallow plowing (which disturbs only the topsoil), subsoiling (which lifts the soil but

does not invert it), and other forms of conservation tillage. In Argentina, one-third of arable land is cultivated using the no-tillage method. No-till is growing in the United States, too. About 23 percent of cropland in the United States is under no-till.

The Nature of Soil

The thin soil that covers Earth is very variable in quality and depth. In some areas, it is only 1 inch (3 cm) deep. In others, it may be as much as 66 feet (20 m) deep. Only about one-third of the soil on Earth's surface can be used for agriculture. The rest is locked under the polar icecaps, on mountains, or in other inaccessible places, making it useless to farmers. Even the soil that is available is of vastly differing value. Less than 10 percent is truly fertile. Most soil needs effort and careful management to be consistently productive.

The process of soil formation begins with the weathering of parent rock to produce a layer of loose material known as **regolith**. Further weathering and the addition of decayed organic matter, living organisms, water, and air give rise to a material (effectively topsoil) that can support plant growth.

Most soil needs effort and careful management to be consistently productive.

The rock constituents of soil are of three basic types—sand, silt, and clay—classified according to size. Particles more than 0.8 inches (2 mm) in diameter are classified as stones and are not part of true soil, though stones often make up a high proportion of the earth mass in a typical field.

The international scale is as follows, based on the diameter of a particle:

sand–between 0.8 and 0.0008 inches (2.0 and 0.02 mm)

silt–between 0.0008 and 0.00008 inches (0.02 and 0.002 mm)

clay–less than 0.00008 inches (0.002 mm)

Sand may be further classified into coarse sand—between 0.8 and 0.008 inches (2.0 and 0.2 mm), and fine sand—between 0.008 and 0.0008 inches (0.2 and 0.02 mm). The proportions of these basic

Earthworms consume plant debris and release nutrient-rich waste that keeps soil healthy.

materials in a soil determine its texture and its ability to take up moisture, air, and nutrients.

More than two-thirds of Earth's rock is made from just three minerals—feldspar (about 51 percent), quartz (12 percent), and mica (5 percent). The weathering of quartz produces sands and silts, while weathering of mica and feldspar produces clays.

Earthworms have an important function in aerating the soil and maintaining its fertility.

Rocks have a mixture of minerals, and soils have a mixture of clay, silt, and sand. Clay soils, of which there are various types, tend to be rich in nutrients, but they are heavy to work, and they are prone to waterlogging or cracking. Sandy soils are easy to cultivate, being light and well-drained. They have easy root penetration, but they lack the quality of **adsorption** that enables nutrients to stick to clay. Sandy soils tend to require a heavier use of fertilizers. Silty soils also tend to lack mineral and organic nutrients, and may be subject to clogging and surface runoff.

Loam is often regarded as the ideal agricultural soil. With a 20 percent clay content, it can hold moisture and nutrients, but with 40 percent sand, it also

SIZE OF SOIL PARTICLES

The relative sizes of the three basic soil particles illustrate the large difference between clay (1), silt (30), and sand (1,000). The texture of a soil depends on the proportion of these three basic mineral ingredients. The clay fraction is particularly important in determining fertility. Adsorption of nutrients depends largely on the surface area and electric charging properties of clay-sized minerals. Soil acidity is another key factor in determining fertility, since adsorption by iron oxides varies with the pH value of the soil.

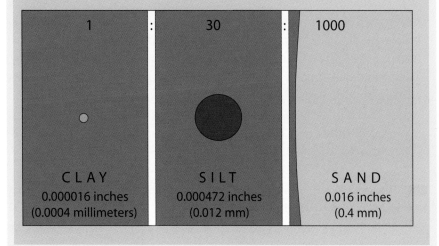

1	:	30	:	1000
C L A Y		S I L T		S A N D
0.000016 inches		0.000472 inches		0.016 inches
(0.0004 millimeters)		(0.012 mm)		(0.4 mm)

has good drainage and aeration. The remaining 40 percent silt content holds the clay and sand together. Loam provides an easily worked soil that is fertile and resistant to erosion.

The classification of soils is a complex business, and there is no agreed international system. Soil type depends not only on the parent rock, but also on climate and topography. Thus, soil on a steep slope is different from soil in the river valley below it. The soil of the tropics is different from the soil of the tundra or the prairies.

Natural soil nutrients are derived partly from minerals in rock particles and partly from humus. Moisture and air and the action of microorganisms in the clay/humus mixture enable these nutrients to be taken up by plants.

Earthworms, whose combined activities can turn over as much as 18 tons per acre (40 t per h) of soil each year, have an important function in aerating the soil and thus maintaining its fertility. A similar role is performed by termites in the tropics. Most soil organisms live in the top 8 inches (20 cm) of soil. They can be killed or damaged by excessive use of pesticides and even by fertilizers, though the latter can, of course, make up some of the deficiency.

SOIL PH

A measurement of how acidic or basic objects are is called pH. This is measured using a pH scale between 0 and 14. Acidic objects have a pH between 0 and 7, such as lemon juice and battery acid. Basic objects (also called alkaline), such as seawater and bleach, have a pH between 7 and 14. Pure water is neutral, or 7, on the pH scale.

The pH of a soil solution is important because the solution carries in it nutrients such as nitrogen, potassium, and phosphorus. Plants need these in specific amounts to grow, thrive, and fight off diseases. If the pH of the soil solution is increased above 5.5, nitrogen is made available to plants. If the pH of the solution is between 6 and 7, phosphorus is available.

If the soil solution is too acidic, plants cannot use nitrogen, potassium, phosphorus, and other nutrients. Plants will absorb toxic metals, and some plants eventually will die of poisoning. Soil becomes acidic for many reasons. One reason is the dribbling away of rainwater. This can carry away basic ions, such as calcium, magnesium, potassium, and sodium. Soil can also become acidic when carbon dioxide forms from decomposing organic matter and **root respiration** dissolving in soil water. This can make a weak organic acid. As well, soil can become acidic due to the formation of strong organic and inorganic acids from decaying organic matter and the oxidation of fertilizers.

■■ High soil acidity is harmful to many plant species. Rhododendrons are resistant to high acidity and grow best in areas that have slightly acidic soil.

THE LIVING SOIL

Healthy soil teems with life. Thirty-five cubic feet (1 cubic meter) of good soil might contain the following biomass.

50 g	= 1.8 oz	10 g	= 0.4 oz	2 g	= 0.07 oz	4.5 g	= 0.2 oz
100 g	= 3.5 oz	0.01 g	= 0.0003 oz	0.2 g	= 0.007 oz	1.5 g	= 0.05 oz
1 g	= 0.03 oz	0.6	= 0.02 oz	0.5 g	= 0.02 oz	40 g	= 1.4 oz

Microflora

1,000,000,000,000 Bacteria

10,000,000,000 Actinomycetes

1,000,000,000 Fungi

1,000,000 Algae

   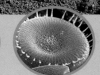

Bacteria 50g   **Actinomycetes** 50g   **Fungi** 100g   **Algae** 1g

Microfauna

500,000,000,000 Flagellates

100,000,000,000 Rhizopods

1,000,000 Ciliates

Flagellates 10g   **Rhizopods** 10g   **Ciliates** 10g

Small Soil Animals

25,000 Rotifers

1,000,000 Nematodes

100,000 Mites

50,000 Springtails

Rotifers 0.01g   **Nematodes** 1g   **Mites** 1g   **Springtails** 0.6g

Larger Soil Animals

10,000 Potworms

50 Slugs & Snails

50 Spiders

50 Woodlice

300 Centipedes

100 Beetles & Larve

100 Fly Larve

80 Earthworms

150 Other Insects

Potworms 2g   **Slugs & Snails** 1g   **Spiders** .2g   **Woodlice** 0.5g

 (Centipedes) (Beetles & Larvae) (Fly Larve) (Earthworms)

Centipedes 4.5g   **Beetles & Larvae** 1.5g   **Fly Larve** 1g   **Earthworms** 40g

Modern nitrogen fertilizers are often used to assist with crop growth. However, chemicals from nitrogen fertilizers can leak into water runoff and groundwater.

KEY CONCEPTS

Fertilizers Farmers have always used fertilizers to enrich the soil and improve plant growth. Before the **Industrial Revolution**, all farming was organic and depended on the recycling principle. Animal manure and dead plants were plowed back into the soil, adding nutrients while getting rid of unwanted waste. Sometimes artificial fertilizers were used, but they were made from potash and **guano**, not chemicals. Though nitrogen occurs naturally, artificially produced nitrogen compounds, such as nitrates and urea, have proved to be effective fertilizers, and their discovery transformed agriculture. It meant that crop production could be increased with the use of chemicals. Modern fertilizers provide the soil with nitrogen, potassium, and phosphorus. Though these elements are now considered essential, soil fertility depends on many other factors, such as the number of microorganisms and worms.

Runoff After precipitation falls to Earth, it begins to move in accordance with the laws of gravity. Some precipitation is absorbed by the ground, but most of it flows downhill as runoff. Runoff amounts are affected by several factors, including soil type, elevation, slope, and vegetation. Runoff from cultivated land often carries excess nutrients, which ultimately can degrade water quality.

Duties: Collects and analyzes soil samples and recommends actions to promote soil health and conservation

Education: Bachelor or master of science degree in agricultural science, soil science, or a related discipline

Interests: Problem solving, the outdoors, environmental conservation, data analysis, puzzles

To find out more about a career in soil science, navigate to **www.uwyo.edu/Range MGT/Renewable_Pages/ Programs/soils/ soilscientist.html** or try **http://sails.usda.gov/ education/facts/ careers.html**

Careers in Focus

Soil scientists study the relationship of soil to the climate and the environment. They examine soil as a medium for growth of economically important plants, as a support for ecosystems, as a body for supporting buildings, and as a depository for pollutants.

Soil scientists look at soil both in the field and in the laboratory. They have a solid scientific background, as well as an understanding of environmental issues. Soil scientists use well-developed analytical skills to collect and analyze data, perform computer modeling, and interpret soil data in reports and studies.

Soil scientists work in many different areas. Some study specific topics, such as the effects of fossil fuel emissions on soil, moisture content, or soil fertility. Some are microbiologists who study microbes in the soil and their effect on soil fertility. Pedologists are soil scientists who classify soil and prepare soil maps. They rate soil according to its suitability for various uses. Some soil scientists determine the best soils to use to store waste to avoid environmental contamination. Others examine contaminated soil and find ways to restore it. Some soil scientists work with government agencies to determine how land should be used, and others work to prevent soil loss and erosion in specified areas. All soil scientists use their knowledge of soil composition to make judgments, evaluate the use of soil, and to manage soil for future use.

Soil Erosion

Rainfall and wind carry away billions of tons of Earth's topsoil every year. The result of this huge loss is not only a reduction in the productive capacity of the farms that lose the soil but also other costs arising from the silting up of irrigation systems, water purification plants, dams, and reservoirs. In some countries, such as Costa Rica, Malawi, and Mexico, the total losses in productive potential attributable to soil depletion may amount to 0.5–1.5 percent of gross domestic product (GDP) each year. In the United States, the cost of damage from waterborne sediments may exceed $10 billion a year.

The causes of soil erosion are many. The action of wind and water moves particles of soil without any intervention from humans. Heavy rainfall washes soil into rivers that may transfer it for thousands of miles to the sea. Contaminated soil carries its toxicity into the sea where it can damage aquatic plants and animals.

Poor farming methods are the main causes of soil erosion. Often, there is the removal of vegetative cover that binds the soil through the root systems of grass, other plants, and trees. Vegetation also absorbs some of the Sun's heat and protects the soil from the direct impact of heavy rainfall. Remove the vegetation, and the soil is easily whisked away by the first downpour or gust of wind.

Poor farming methods are the main causes of soil erosion today.

Some farming problems include **overgrazing** of sparsely vegetated land, where nothing can grow properly because every new shoot is eaten as soon as it shows its head above ground. Overgrazing in some countries is the result of overpopulation. In others, it occurs because of intensive farming. In Africa, for example, more animals may be needed to feed growing families from the same area of land. In Australia, livestock farming in semiarid areas has exacerbated the problem of desertification. Worldwide, overgrazing accounts for more than one-third of all soil degradation through erosion and desertification.

Deforestation is another cause of soil erosion. Recent estimates place current global forest cover at about 50 percent of its original extent, with a large proportion of this loss having occurred within the past 50 years. Though public attention has focused on rain forest destruction, all types of trees are involved in soil retention, and their loss contributes to erosion. Deforestation is worst in Latin America (especially Brazil), Southeast Asia (especially Indonesia), and central Africa (especially the Democratic Republic of Congo).

The extensive use of slash and burn techniques in the tropics can quickly produce areas of desert, since the soil left behind after the trees are cut down is usually thin and of poor quality. After two or three years, the plot is abandoned by the farmer who moves to a new area. Small clearings can be healed by new growth, but larger areas become so depleted that nothing can be sustained. The thin soil is soon washed away, leaving desertification in its wake.

■■■ Farms may become unsustainable if too much soil erosion occurs.

devastating when steep wooded slopes are involved. Water rushing down a treeless mountainside quickly removes all usable soil from the valley. For example, fertile soil from the hills of Nepal is transferred by river onto the flood plains of Bangladesh. Fresh alluvial deposits are often welcome to the farmers on the receiving end, but it is a disaster for those at higher altitudes who lose their best soil. Trees and other vegetation also act as windbreaks, thereby reducing the amount of soil that is blown from the top of fields by the wind. Loess is a fine windblown soil that can be very fertile if it lands in the right place (as on the plains of northern China). For the most part, however, wind erosion dissipates the topsoil in such a way that it is lost to agriculture.

is a vital aspect of soil protection worldwide. Whether trees are cut down for the lumber trade, to clear land for farming or livestock, or to provide fuel for cooking and heating, the impact is the same—erosion and further impoverishment of the land.

For the most part, wind erosion dissipates the topsoil in such a way that it is lost to agriculture.

The problem of erosion is not confined to the Third World. About 16 percent of the total land area of Europe is threatened with erosion. In the United States, large areas of agricultural land are at risk of erosion and need careful control measures. The creation of the American dust bowl in the

destroy farmland over a large area.

The use of irrigation in farming has increased strongly in recent decades. Traditional small-scale water wheels and ditches have been supplemented by large schemes that may combine hydroelectric dams, as well. It is important that irrigation is carefully managed.

In hot climates, rapid evaporation causes salts to be drawn to the surface. Poor practices have led to almost one-quarter of all irrigated land worldwide being affected by salinization. Further problems are caused by waterlogging and consequent acidification of the soil. Acid rain is still a serious problem in some countries. In western Europe, however, acid rain damage has been cut in half since controls on fossil fuel emissions were introduced in the 1980s.

SOIL DEGRADATION

Soil productivity is affected by the deterioration of physical, chemical, and biological soil properties. The United Nations Environment Programme (UNEP) has summarized the types and causes of soil degradation. Soil quality is dependent on the degree of soil degradation processes, land use, and management practices.

Types		Causes	
Water erosion	56%	Overgrazing	35%
Wind erosion	28%	Deforestation	30%
Chemical degradation	12%	Agriculture	27%
Physical degradation	4%	Overexploitation of vegetation	7%
		Industrial activity	1%

Simple techniques, such as contour cultivation, grass hedging, and tree planting, can reduce erosion by 50 percent. Mulching, manuring, and low tillage also cut down erosion and, at the same time, increase the fertility of the soil.

If removal of vegetation is a primary cause of soil erosion, it follows that replacing the vegetation is the best solution. The most suitable measures depend upon local terrain and climate, but typically, they include the planting of trees, bushes, or grasses to provide windbreaks and improve water retention.

Contouring—the planting of crops along hill contours rather than up and down the slopes—greatly reduces erosion. In India, contour ditches have helped to quadruple the survival chances of tree seedlings and quintuple their early growth. Use is also being made of vetiver grass "hedges" planted in contour strips across hill slopes. Vetiver grass has deep roots and helps to bind the soil, dramatically reducing erosion. Other types of grass have also been used in similar ways in other parts of the world, such as Indonesia and the Philippines. In the Sahel region of Africa, where water is too scarce for such methods, rock embankments, constructed along contour lines, have been shown to increase yields by 10 percent in average years and by 50 percent in dry seasons.

Mulching fields with the waste matter from harvested crops or other material (varying from sawdust to black plastic) keeps the ground moist, reduces erosion, and feeds the soil. Mulching can both reduce erosion and increase crop yields.

"Cover crops" are useful in providing green manure, as well as protection from erosion. Cover crops are grown to serve various conservation functions other than harvest and sale. Another technique that helps to reduce erosion and keep soil fertile is the practice of "alley cropping." Long carried out in Mediterranean countries, alley cropping involves contour planting crops between rows of trees.

■ In Afghanistan, dust storms occur because there is not enough vegetation to hold soil together and prevent erosion.

Sheet and **rill** erosion often occur together, removing soil layers from the land surface by the action of rainfall and runoff. Sheet and rill erosion is the first stage in water erosion. Wind erosion is the process of detachment, transport, and deposition of soil by wind.

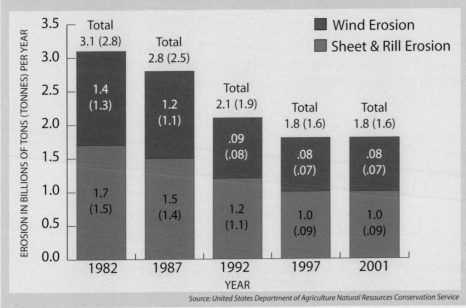

Wind Erosion
Sheet & Rill Erosion

Soil erosion on cropland decreased from 3.1 billion tons (2.8 billion t) per year in 1982 to 1.8 billion tons (1.6 billion t) per year in 2001. In this time period, sheet and rill erosion dropped by almost 41 percent, while wind erosion dropped by 43 percent.

Source: United States Department of Agriculture Natural Resources Conservation Service

KEY CONCEPTS

Deforestation Deforestation is the cutting down of forests for forest products, or to clear land for agriculture, construction, or other human activities. Many international organizations use more specific definitions of deforestation.

Gross Domestic Product (GDP) The gross domestic product is the total value of goods produced and services provided in a country in one year. GDP is used to measure the wealth of a country. However, Some economists argue that GDP does not tell the whole story. For example, GDP measures the total amount of lumber sold, but it does not account for the environmental damage caused by logging.

Intensive Farming Intensive farming methods allow a rather small number of people to produce vast quantities of food. Energy, money, and production methods are concentrated on a particular crop or animal, and such specialization generally results in very high output. Technology, in the form of chemicals, genetic engineering, and hormones, is used to maximize output. Intensive farming is highly efficient in the short term, producing as much food as possible as cheaply as possible. Intensive farming is the norm in the developed world and increasingly common in the developing world.

Irrigation Irrigation is the practice of moving water from a river or storage area across land. Some areas that receive insufficient amounts of rainfall are irrigated to grow crops. Irrigation has been practiced for thousands of years around the world.

Slash and Burn Slash and burn agriculture is a method of land clearing. Trees and other vegetation are cut down and burned in order to clear the land. The ash acts as a fertilizer and adds nutrients to the soil, which is then planted.

Born: 1940 in Nyeri, Kenya

Legacy: Founded the Green Belt Movement to work toward the empowerment of women through tree planting and erosion control in rural Kenya

Navigate to **http://greenbelt movement.org/w.php?id=3** for more information about Wangari Maathai and the Green Belt Movement.

People in Focus

Dr. Wangari Maathai studied biological science in the United States, Germany, and Kenya. In 1971, she earned a Ph.D. in veterinary medicine from the University of Nairobi. Maathai was the first woman in eastern and central Africa to earn a doctoral degree. She was also the first woman to teach veterinary anatomy at the University of Nairobi.

As a biological scientist, Maathai understands the damaging effects of soil erosion. She joined the National Council of Women of Kenya in 1976, and through her council work, she explored the idea of using reforestation to help the cause of women in Kenya. Wangari Maathai founded the Green Belt Movement in 1977. This movement seeks to resolve the social and environmental problems caused by deforestation. Women establish small tree nurseries

in rural areas and local workers are paid to tend the trees. The seedlings are given to rural people who prove they are willing and capable of caring for the trees. They are then paid for the number of trees that survive. In addition to stopping erosion, tree planting provides a sustainable source of wood fuel and an income to rural Kenyans. The Green Belt Movement has expanded to over 30 countries in Africa and also has an international chapter.

Maathai's work for political change in Kenya has been successful. She was elected to Kenya's parliament in 2002, and she was appointed assistant minister for environment, natural resources, and wildlife. She has received many awards, including the Africa Prize for her work in preventing hunger.

In 2004, Maathai was awarded the Nobel Peace Prize for "her contribution to sustainable development, democracy and peace"—the first African woman to receive the award.

Soil Contamination

The use of inorganic fertilizers with new high-yielding grains has transformed agricultural production over the past 60 years. World fertilizer use increased from 14 million tons in 1950 to 145 in 2003.

Fertilizers fall into three main groups, supplying the three most basic mineral needs of plants—nitrogen, phosphorus, and potassium. Some fertilizers are naturally produced, such as the Strassfurt potash deposits in Germany. Most inorganic fertilizers are

---

The use of fertilizers has often been encouraged by government subsidies.

---

artificially manufactured by companies in the industrial chemicals sector.

Consumption of fertilizers in developed countries has stabilized. In some countries, consumption is decreasing as environmental concerns increase and efficiency of application improves. Since the 1980s, consumption has doubled in the developing world, where the use of fertilizers has often been encouraged by government **subsidies**. In Indonesia, for example, farmers only pay one-third of the world price,

▬▬▬ Agrochemicals can harm the environment if they are improperly used. Lead, arsenic, nickel, and other materials can cause soil contamination and harm plants and animals.

with subsidies covering the rest of the cost. World consumption of fertilizers in 2000 was 90 million tons (82 million t) of nitrogenous fertilizer, 36 million tons (33 million t) of phosphatic fertilizer, and 24 million tons (22 million t) of potash.

There is no doubt that fertilizers can increase crop yields dramatically, but accurate measurement of the exact amount required is difficult. To make sure that enough fertilizer is applied, most farmers use more than is necessary. As a result, a large amount is wasted.

Plants only take what they need. The rest (which may be as much as half of the original application) remains in the soil or is lost through leaching or runoff. Some of the residue is filtered into the water supply. Among environmentalists, concern over nitrate has been growing. It has been estimated that one-quarter of the citizens of the European community are supplied with drinking water that has nitrate levels above the recommended maximum level of 0.002 ounces per quart (50 mg per liter). Fertilizer that flows into rivers, lakes, and coastal waters can also cause a buildup of algal growth that suffocates aquatic plants and animals, called eutrophication.

The application to fields of sewage sludge and livestock slurry has also caused problems, particularly when this takes place in winter and the ground is too

AGROCHEMICALS-BOTH BOON AND BANE

Farmers have used chemicals for centuries, but it is only since World War II that the agrochemical industry has increased. Apart from the big three of plant nutrition—nitrogen, phosphorus, and potassium—at least 10 other trace minerals are needed, including sulfur, calcium, and magnesium. Natural soil rarely provides all that is required for large-scale agricultural production. Hence, it is usually necessary to add artificial supplements. As far as the plants are concerned, it makes no difference whether a particular nutrient is supplied by nature or by industry.

Weed control has always presented a big challenge to farmers and was the cause of much drudgery in past years, when regular hoeing was the only answer. The development of herbicides was therefore widely welcomed, along with the invention of new chemicals to control insect pests, rodents, fungi, and parasites, for example. Yet the widespread and indiscriminate use of such chemicals proved damaging both to farming ecosystems and human health. Modern pesticides are designed to break down quickly after contact with the soil, but some, such as paraquat, can persist for more than a year.

There is no doubt that fertilizers can increase crop yields dramatically, but accurate measurement of the exact amount required is difficult.

hard to absorb the nutrients. Other concerns include the transfer of diseases through the water system when slurry or sewage waste is washed into rivers or irrigation channels.

Pesticides have substantially increased farming productivity. For example, today, tending 2.5 acres (1 h) of maize takes only one-sixth of the labor required before chemical weedkillers were introduced. Herbicides account for almost half of all pesticides sold. Insecticides account for a further 25–30 percent of the market, the rest being taken up by fungicides and other specialist chemicals. Each year, more than 2.8 million tons (2.5 million t) of toxic pesticide chemicals are applied to the world's farmland. Inevitably, traces of these toxins collect in food and water.

Though pesticides have often reduced labor costs and improved yields, they have not succeeded in defeating the various afflictions suffered by crops. Many crops, particularly in the tropics, still suffer heavy losses, despite the array of sophisticated chemicals that are sprayed upon them.

As with fertilizers, farmers tend to use more pesticide than is necessary. In developed countries, fruits and vegetables are often sprayed to ensure good cosmetic appearance and prevent skin blemishes that would substantially reduce the selling price. Such "insurance" spraying is widely practiced on other crops to prevent pest outbreaks that reduce yield.

Particularly in developing countries that receive heavy government subsidies, pesticides are often used incorrectly, with subsequent dangers to the health of humans and livestock. In fact, pesticides are much safer and more targeted than they were in the past. Nevertheless, they still depend on the use of poisons that inhibit or destroy the life systems of plants or insects. Since human chemistry is very

---

Agrochemicals have already damaged the soil and contaminated drinking water.

---

similar, it is likely that some pesticides can harm humans, too. The risks, however, have be weighed against the benefits.

The awareness of these problems has lead to a growing interest in techniques such as integrated pest management (IPM). IPM uses a variety of methods to control pests, including the release of specialist parasites or sterile males to control insect populations. In one program, the introduction of natural predators reduced cassava mealybug infestations in Africa, with a cost-benefit ratio of nearly 150 to 1. Another approach that is being used with more and more success is **bioengineering** of pest-resistant (and herbicide-resistant) crops.

Since nature adapts to changing circumstances, such control efforts can never succeed completely. New pests and diseases appear as the old ones are defeated. A solution based on using larger quantities of stronger chemicals would be disastrous in the long term and even more injurious to human health. After all, agrochemicals have already damaged the soil and contaminated drinking water, even in strictly regulated environments such as Europe and North America.

MAIN SOIL CONTAMINANTS LISTED BY U.S. ENVIRONMENTAL PROTECTION AGENCY (EPA)

The EPA maintains a list of several hundred chemicals that are considered extremely hazardous or acutely toxic. The more common are: acetone, arsenic, barium, benzene, cadmium, chloroform, cyanide, lead, mercury, polychlorinated biphenyls (PCBs), tetrachloroethylene, toluene, and trichloroethylene (TCE).

Sources of chemical contamination that can damage soil include spillage from petroleum products, industrial waste, and cumulative pesticide use.

■ Pesticides are sprayed on crops to ward off plant-eating insects. However, they also kill insects that are beneficial to crops, such as the ladybug, a predator that eats insect pests that are harmful to crops.

PESTICIDE TYPES

Pesticides fall into various chemical categories, including organochlorines (e.g., aldrin, chlordane, DDT, lindane); organophosphates (e.g., diazinon, glyphosate, malathion, parathion); phenoxyacetic acids (e.g., 2,4,5-T and 2,4-D); carbamates (e.g., aldicarb, carbaryl); and pyrethroids. Many of these chemicals are regarded as potentially dangerous to public health and are subject to national rules on toxic releases. Some are regarded as especially risky, being "persistent, bioaccumulative, and toxic" (PBT).

Half of all agrochemicals are used on five key crops—cereals, maize, rice, soya, and cotton.

In 2004, U.S. cotton producers spent and average of $60 on pesticides per planted acre (0.4 ha) of cotton.

Cotton farmers are particularly heavy users of pesticides. There is also a large and growing market for nonagricultural pesticides in homes, gardens, golf courses, and turf management.

KEY CONCEPTS

Eutrophication
Eutrophication is the enrichment of an ecosystem with chemical nutrients, typically compounds containing nitrogen, phosphorus, or both. The increase in available nutrients promotes plant growth, favoring certain species over others and forcing a change in species composition. In aquatic environments, enhanced growth of choking aquatic vegetation or phytoplankton (that is, an algal bloom) disrupts normal functioning of the ecosystem.

Pesticides Pesticides are used to prevent, destroy, or control pests, including mice, insects, fungi, weeds, and bacteria. Many household products, such as rat poison and disinfectants, are considered pesticides, though pesticides are usually associated with the protection of crops. Overuse can lead to resistance on the part of pests, and because most pesticides are chemicals and therefore toxic, they are often dangerous to humans, animals, and the environment. Concern over such risks has led to the development and increased use of biologically-based pesticides, which are generally safer than traditional pesticides, though still not without risk.

Intensive Agriculture

Intensive agriculture is really a contradiction in terms. After all, the word "agriculture" means caring for the land. Traditionally, this involved matching inputs with outputs in order to preserve the long-term fertility of the soil. Intensive farming involves getting maximum output from minimum input in order to produce both food and profit in the largest possible amounts. It is a form of nutrient mining where the capital resource of the soil is depleted.

The factory farming approach, whether applied to crops or livestock, has come under increasing fire because it treats animals as conveyor belt products rather than as living creatures. This approach to farming also damages the land. In a traditional mixed farm, a variety of livestock and crops were rotated in such a way that the balance of the soil was conserved year after year. Inputs equaled outputs, and the balance of nature was maintained. In the short term, a large farm concentrating on a single crop can produce that crop much more cheaply than a small mixed farm. Thus small-scale mixed farming, which was kind to the soil, has been driven out by large-scale monoculture, which almost always damages the soil in the long term.

> ## Intensive farming involves getting maximum output from minimum input.

The use of tractors and other forms of heavy machinery have compressed the soil over large areas and reduced its capacity to absorb moisture and air. Plant roots find it more difficult to penetrate compacted soil, and the processes of chemical and biological change that maintain nutrient levels are slowed down. Compaction is thought to affect about half of all intensively cultivated row-crops in the United States. At the same time, deep plowing upsets soil structure and loosens topsoil, making it more vulnerable to erosion.

The use of big farming machines leads to larger field sizes and the removal of impediments, such as

■ Factory farming of livestock often includes large amounts of fertilizer to produce feed and a large production of organic waste that cannot be absorbed by the soil.

Before the introduction of farming machinery in the 1900s, farming was often done in small strips. Today, strip farming is once again gaining popularity because it prevents soil erosion and increases the soil's ability to sustain crops.

undergrowth, hedgerows, and trees. Instead of small areas of land anchored by the surrounding vegetation, there are giant open fields. In the dry season, winds blow across these open expanses and lift off the topsoil.

Many farmers are beginning to realize the scale of the damage being done. Yet even those who would like to break out of this pattern of farming are finding it difficult to do so. Though more conservationist policies are being adopted, true organic farming is practiced on about 64 million acres (26 million h) worldwide and accounts for barely two percent of global food sales.

Frequently, government incentives have had the effect of encouraging large-scale farming and monocropping. Market forces operate on a short-term basis. Although there is a premium on organically grown food in developed countries, this does not apply to most of the world. Cheap food is the main requirement in the poorer

> *Although there is a premium on organically grown food in developed countries, this does not apply in most of the world.*

countries of the world. To meet the increasing demand for food, intensive large-scale agriculture is bound to continue. Yet pressure is building for new management methods that will reduce environmental damage.

Fertilizer use in the European Union (EU) is declining as crop and soil management techniques improve. According to a report from the European Fertilizer Manufacturers Association (EFMA), EU farmers will be using 20 percent less nitrogen, 50 percent less phosphorus, and 40 percent less potassium in 2010 than they did in the 1980s, when overuse was common. Concern over nitrate runoff led the EU to introduce restrictions on the use of nitrogen fertilizer in 1991. These measures reduced environmental damage, but made it difficult for farmers to maintain production levels. For example, Denmark, once renowned for its fertile soils, has become a net importer of wheat because its farmers can no longer produce enough good quality wheat to meet domestic demand.

Inorganic fertilizers provide half of all nutrients in European agriculture, the rest coming from livestock manures and municipal and industrial wastes. Most of the nutrients in manure must be mineralized by microbial action before they can be taken up by plants. Chemical fertilizers have the advantage that they can be applied in measured doses at critical points in plant growth, thereby maximizing crop yield. Soil characteristics vary even across a single piece of land. Modern farmers now have the benefit of geopositioning

> *Chemical fertilizers have the advantage that they can be applied in measured doses at critical points in plant growth, thereby maximizing crop yield.*

(geographical positioning) technology that enables them to link dosages of fertilizer or pesticide to different areas of the same field, greatly increasing the efficiency of applications while also preventing waste and potentially harmful runoff.

Other useful technologies include computer-controlled irrigation and roller systems that make small indentations in the surface of a freshly sown field, creating miniature reservoirs that help to conserve water and direct it more evenly to individual plants. Bioengineering is, of course, another technology that seems likely to transform agriculture in the future. Its impact on soil biodiversity could be critical.

PESTICIDE USE

The United States is the world's biggest user of pesticides, applying about 386 million tons (350 million t) to the land in 1997 (more than 10 times as much as Great Britain, where agriculture is also highly industrialized). U.S. consumption included 235,000 tons (213,000 t) of weedkiller, 123,000 tons (112,000 t) of insecticide, and 26,000 tons (24,000 t) of fungicides and bactericides.

The Food and Agriculture Organization of the United Nations (FAO) has only limited statistics on pesticide use in developing countries. Pakistan reported using more than 111,000 tons (10,000 t) of pesticide in 1998. Insecticides alone accounted for 10,400 tons (9,419 t) of these chemcials. This figure is a reflection of the serious problem caused by insect pests in hot countries.

Despite the FAO's support for nonchemical systems such as integrated pest management, figures for international trade in pesticides have shown a steady increase since 1970. The biggest exporters in 2000 were Germany ($1.8 billion in sales value), France ($1.7 billion), the United States ($1.4 billion), and Great Britain ($1.2 billion).

■ Crop dusting uses airplanes to spread pesticides over large fields.

WORLD TRADE IN CHEMICAL PESTICIDES (THOUSANDS OF DOLLARS)

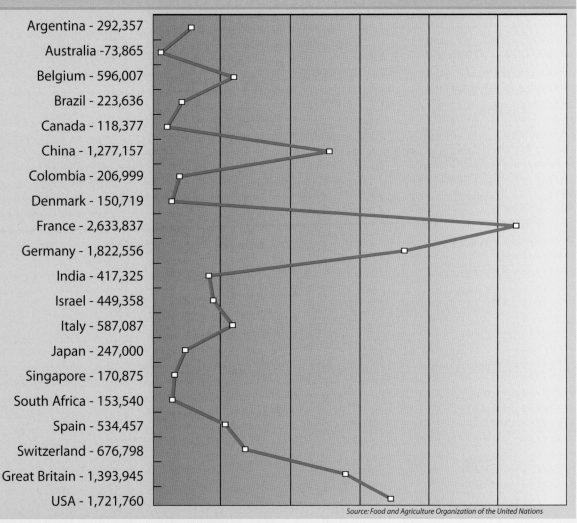

Argentina - 292,357
Australia -73,865
Belgium - 596,007
Brazil - 223,636
Canada - 118,377
China - 1,277,157
Colombia - 206,999
Denmark - 150,719
France - 2,633,837
Germany - 1,822,556
India - 417,325
Israel - 449,358
Italy - 587,087
Japan - 247,000
Singapore - 170,875
South Africa - 153,540
Spain - 534,457
Switzerland - 676,798
Great Britain - 1,393,945
USA - 1,721,760

Source: Food and Agriculture Organization of the United Nations

Dengue fever is a type of viral disease transmitted to humans by the Aedes Aegypti mosquito. In emergency situations, governments must sometimes spray pesticides to reduce the Aedes Aegypti mosquito population.

WORLD FERTILIZER CONSUMPTION

World fertilizer use has risen steadily in the developing world since the 1960s but has declined in the industrial world since the 1980s. China accounted for 27 percent of global fertilizer use in 2000. The three basic fertilizer types, based on nitrogen, phosphorus, and potassium, can increase crop yields substantially, although their overuse can lead to unbalanced soils and contamination of water supply.

Country	Fertilizer Consumption pounds per acre (kg per h)		Index of Food Production (per head 1979-81=100)
	1970/71	1989/90	1988-90
Bangladesh	14.1 (15.7)	89.4 (99.3)	86.4 (96)
China	36.9 (41.0)	235.7 (261.9)	119.7 (133)
Egypt	118.1 (131.2)	363.9 (404.3)	106.2 (118)
Germany	346 (384.4)	333.5 (370.5)	100.8 (112)
Great Britain	236.8 (263.1)	315.2 (350.2)	94.5 (105)
India	12.3 (13.7)	61.8 (68.7)	107.1 (119)
Indonesia	12 (13.3)	104.9 (116.6)	110.7 (123)
Japan	319.2 (354.7)	376.1 (417.9)	90.9 (101)
Malawi	4.7 (5.2)	20.4 (22.7)	74.7 (83)
Netherlands	674.4 (749.3)	578.2 (642.4)	99.9 (111)
Nigeria	0.2 (0.2)	10.9 (12.1)	95.4 (106)
Pakistan	13.1 (14.6)	80.1 (89.0)	90.9 (101)
Philippines	25.8 (28.7)	60.7 (67.4)	75.6 (84)
USA	73.4 (81.6)	88.7 (98.5)	82.8 (92)

Source: The World Bank

Biological engineering is a broad-based discipline that deals with bio-molecular and molecular processes, product design, sustainability and analysis of biological systems. Bioengineering has recently been helpful in solving problems in agriculture that go beyond those fertilization or pesticide use. For instance, irrigation, an almost universal necessity in agriculture, slowly raises the salinity of fields. Scientists have recently developed a transgenic tomato plant that can grow in briny soil - soil with a salt content 50 times higher than tomatoes can normally tolerate. The tomato actually reduces the salinity of the soil as it is farmed, reclaiming the fields for re-use and preserving land elsewhere.

However, the practical application of bioengineering is not without its critics. Some say that the long term effects of genetic engineering are still not fully understood, and it is irresponsible to expose the public to genetically engineered crops. They cite the results of the Human Genome Project, a $3 billion study conducted by the National Institutes of Health, which found there are too few human genes to account for the vast inherited differences between people and lower animals or plants, indicating that agents other than DNA must contribute to genetic complexity. Critical scientists claim that under the influence of specialized proteins that carry out "alternative splicing," a single gene can give rise to a variety of different proteins, resulting in more than a single inherited trait per gene. As a result, the gene's effect on inheritance cannot be predicted simply from its chemical composition.

Yet the future of biological engineering remains to be seen. European resistance to crops that have been genetically engineered may be overcome by events. The World Trade Organization ruled in 2006 that a six-year European ban on genetically engineered crops violates international trade rules.

KEY CONCEPTS

Biodiversity Biodiversity refers to the variety of plant, animal, fungus, and microbial species found on Earth and the various ecosystems, or habitats, in which they live. Evolving over time, organisms have become uniquely adapted to particular ecosystems, and the removal or extinction of any one species can have far-reaching and destructive effects. If an ecosystem's delicate balance is upset, air quality, soil quality, and even rainfall can be affected. As habitats are ruined, hundreds of thousands of species—and potential medical cures and nutrient-rich foods— are forever lost.

Factory farming
Factory farms are huge operations where animals are kept confined in close quarters. Some factory farms process millions of animals each year. Feedlots are a typical form of factory farms. Young cattle are brought in and fed grains that promote quick growth. Often, the feed has growth supplements added to further speed up the growing process. On average, cattle remain in feedlots for 120 days, after which they are sent to slaughter.

Global Positioning System
The Global Positioning System, or GPS, is the only fully-functional satellite navigation system. A constellation of more than two dozen GPS satellites broadcasts precise timing signals by radio to GPS receivers, allowing them to accurately determine their location (longitude, latitude, and altitude) in any weather, day or night, any place on Earth. GPS has become a vital global utility, indispensable for modern navigation on land, sea, and air around the world, as well as an important tool for mapmaking, and land surveying.

Geographic Information System (GIS) A geographic information system is a system for creating and managing spatial data and associated attributes. In the strictest sense, it is a computer system capable of integrating, storing, editing, analyzing, sharing, and displaying geographically-referenced information. In a more generic sense, GIS is a "smart map" tool that allows users to create interactive queries (user created searches), analyze the spatial information, and edit data. Geographic positioning systems allow farmers to locate the exact position of features such as soil type, weeds, water holes, boundaries, and obstructions, and GIS systems allow them to analyze and create specific solutions to each location's specific needs.

Mapping Soil Degradation

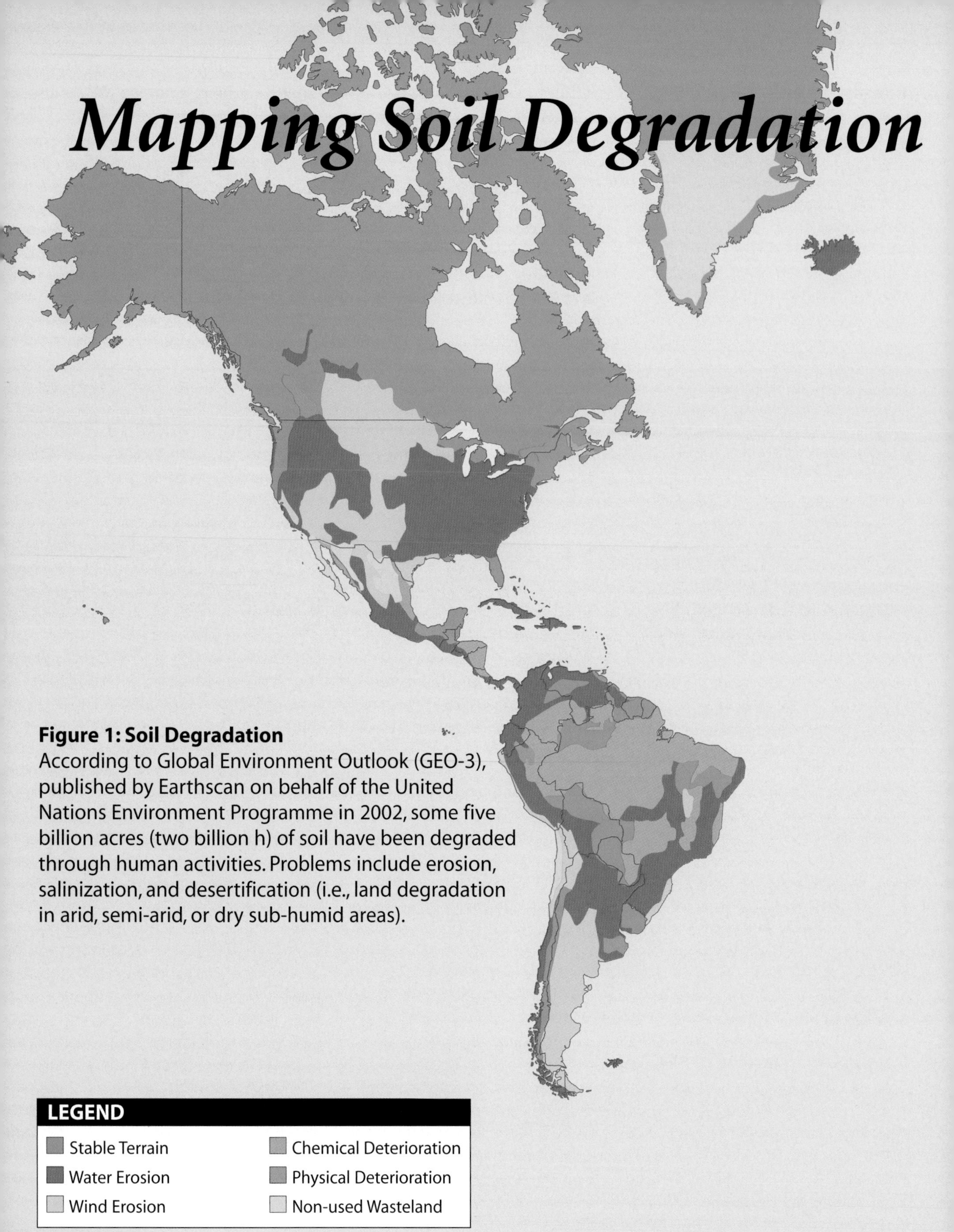

Figure 1: Soil Degradation
According to Global Environment Outlook (GEO-3), published by Earthscan on behalf of the United Nations Environment Programme in 2002, some five billion acres (two billion h) of soil have been degraded through human activities. Problems include erosion, salinization, and desertification (i.e., land degradation in arid, semi-arid, or dry sub-humid areas).

LEGEND

Stable Terrain	Chemical Deterioration
Water Erosion	Physical Deterioration
Wind Erosion	Non-used Wasteland

N

0	1000	2000	3000	miles
0	1,609	3,219	4,828	kilometers

SCALE AT EQUATOR

Source: United Nations Environment Programme, Food and Agriculture Organization of the United Nations

Charting Soil Structure

Figure 2: Soil Nutrients and Pollutants

Nutrients in the soil are derived partly from minerals and partly from organic matter in humus. Minerals are released from humus by the activities of various microorganisms, some of which also help plant roots to take up the nutrients.

Carbon dioxide (CO_2) is absorbed by plants that release oxygen (O_2) back into the atmosphere. Natural bacterial activity and excessive use of nitrogenous fertilizer can release nitrous oxide (N_2O), a greenhouse gas 150 times stronger than carbon dioxide.

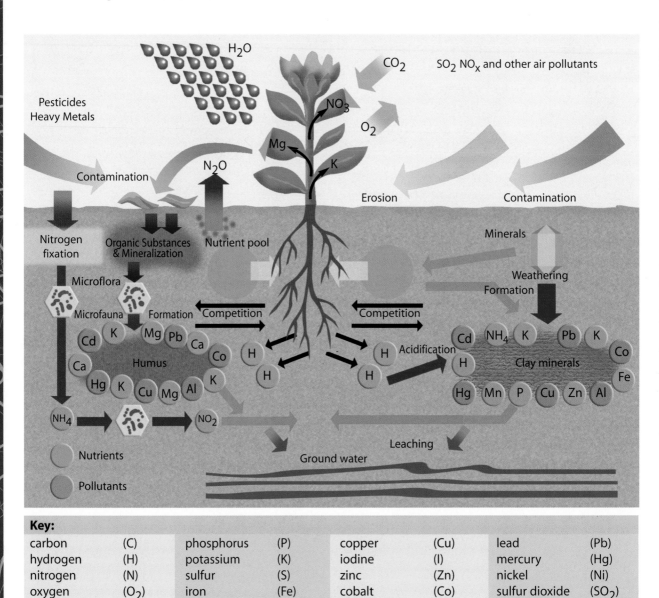

Key:

carbon	(C)	phosphorus	(P)	copper	(Cu)	lead	(Pb)
hydrogen	(H)	potassium	(K)	iodine	(I)	mercury	(Hg)
nitrogen	(N)	sulfur	(S)	zinc	(Zn)	nickel	(Ni)
oxygen	(O_2)	iron	(Fe)	cobalt	(Co)	sulfur dioxide	(SO_2)
calcium	(Ca)	boron	(B)	aluminum	(Al)	nitrogen oxides	(NO_x)
magnesium	(Mg)	manganese	(Mn)	cadmium	(Cd)		

Figure 3: Soil Formation

The development of soils is affected by the nature of the bedrock that forms its basic material, the climate, the lie of the land (hilly and flat terrain absorb water differently, for example), and the plants and animals active in the area. Weathering is more rapid in warm climates with heavy rainfall. Soil formation is very slow in cold tundra regions.

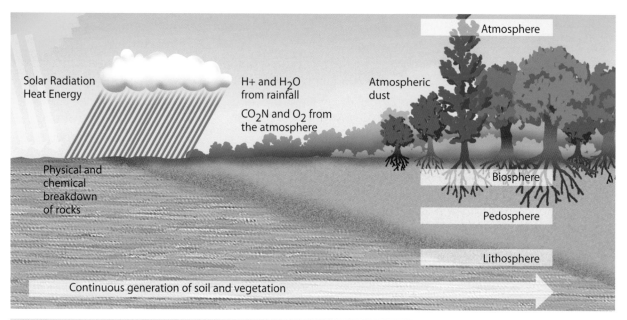

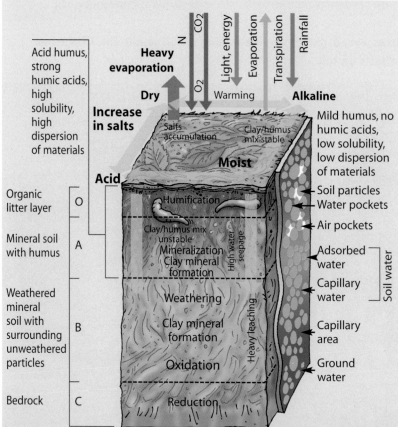

Figure 4: The Soil System

The vertical cross-section, known as the soil profile, shows the division of the soil layers into horizons A, B, C, and O. The top layer of organic litter (O) comprises animal and plant material at various stages of decomposition.

The O and A horizons are where most biological activity takes place and are the most vulnerable to disturbance from chemical or physical intrusion. Fine materials and minerals are carried down to the lower level of horizon B by the action of water seeping through the soil. The bottom layer (horizon C), known as the subsoil, consists of small fragments of weathered rock. It is largely infertile.

Sustainable Agriculture

Intensive farming can lead to soil depletion, contamination, and unhealthy food. Yet the demand for ever increasing quantities of cheap food makes it impossible for agriculture to return to the small mixed farms of the twentieth century. Harking back to the "good old days" of rural life, when half the population was involved in agriculture, will not solve the problem. Science cannot be relied upon to come up soon enough with a new technical fix based on genetic engineering, hydroponics, or plankton, for example. Yet something has to be done to save agriculture from ruining the land upon which it depends.

Among the most important steps that can be taken are greater use of crop rotation and natural methods of fertilization and pest control. The method of plowing or tillage can also have an important effect on soil conservation.

Crop rotation—successive planting of different crops in the same field—is important because it enables the soil to recover between harvests. Planting of deep-rooted legumes, such as alfalfa, for example, draws nutrients to the topsoil. Leguminous crops help in nitrogen fixation, thereby reducing the need for inorganic fertilizer. Rotation also helps to keep crops healthy since pests that feed on one type of plant may not be able to survive on another. Limited crop rotation is already used by many farmers, alternating maize and soya beans, for example. The traditional practice of leaving fallow fields under grass for several years is now relatively rare because of economic considerations, despite the benefits it confers on the

▰▰▰ Depending on the process, tillage can be very useful or very degrading to soil conditions. Tillage has various physical, biological and chemical effects on soil.

soil underneath. Many farmers are under great financial pressure and cannot afford the kind of long-term stewardship that is required—unless government support is available, as in the European Union's set-aside system.

Continuous cropping, though possible with the help of sufficient fertilizers, runs down the soil and becomes more costly each year. It also encourages the development of pests by breaking down the ecological balance that diversity usually provides. Such diversity can be achieved in farming by mosaic cropping in which rows of one crop are interspersed with another, as in a kitchen garden. The mosaic approach is more difficult to manage and mechanize, but is closer to nature's own way of doing things.

One important advantage is that the pest problem tends to be reduced by natural competition. The use of inorganic fertilizers to

---

> *Many farmers are under great financial pressure and cannot afford the kind of long-term stewardship that is required.*

---

feed crops is easy and relatively cheap, but it is not the only way. Animal manure, sewage sludge, garden waste, paper pulp waste, and other natural material can also be used to increase nutrients in soil. The problem is that such wastes are often located in the wrong place. It may not be economical to get them to the fields that need

them. For example, intensive livestock farming produces huge quantities of manure that could be used by cereal farmers, but it may not be worth the effort to transport it to a new location.

In terms of the future prevalence of **sustainable agriculture** in global food production, much will depend on what happens in China, which has 1.2 billion people, and India, which has 90 million small farms and another billion people. Both countries are changing traditional farming practices in order to produce more food. Both are suffering from extensive soil degradation and are acutely aware of the need to adopt sustainable methods.

AGRICULTURE IN CHINA

In China, farmers used sustainable mixed farming methods for centuries. However, most of the population lived in poverty. The country's growing prosperity following industrialization and free-market policies since 1978 has led to a massive change in agriculture. Fertilizer and pesticide use has rocketed. Livestock numbers have grown rapidly to meet rising consumer demand for meat, which China could not afford in the past. Since it takes about 18 pounds (8 kg) of animal feed grain to produce 2 pounds (1 kg) of meat, this change has put extra pressure on land resources. The drive for production has led farmers to overpump wells and exploit marginal lands, exacerbating erosion and desertification. China now faces land degradation on a massive scale.

■■■■ The fertilizing needs of African farmers depend on the crops they are growing, their financial resources, soil quality, and their scale of production.

SOIL LOSS IN AFRICA

Soil degradation is so severe in Africa that many experts fear mass starvation in the future. The UN University Institute for Natural Resources in Africa has warned that, without drastic action to improve soil quality, sub-Saharan Africa will only be able to feed 40 percent of its expected one billion population in 2025.

Most African soils are relatively poor, and their quality has been further downgraded by the removal of vegetative cover for wood fuel or grazing and desertification (which can follow deforestation or cultivation of marginal land). The growing practice of burning animal and crop waste as fuel instead of plowing it back into the soil in order to replace nutrients has also downgraded the soil. These problems have been exacerbated by poor management and a growing population.

Poverty alleviation in Africa will be virtually impossible without improvements in soil quality. The average yield per 2.5 acres (1 h) in sub-Saharan Africa is only a quarter of that achieved in China, partly because African farmers can only afford minimal amounts of fertilizer—9 pounds of fertilizer per acre (10 kg per h), compared with the global average of 40 pounds per acre (46 kg per h).

ZERO TILLAGE AND CONSERVATION AGRICULTURE

The long-established farming practice of soil inversion (for example, tilling the land with a mechanical plow or handheld hoe) has contributed massively to soil erosion and nutrient loss. Exposing soil to the elements—wind, sun, frost, rainfall—makes it vulnerable to erosion and damages soil biodiversity—especially where large fields and monocrops are concerned. Mechanical disturbance of the topsoil plays havoc with soil ecosystems, which, left to themselves, provide a natural form of tillage and recycling. Earthworms and millions of other creatures play a part in keeping soil healthy and fertile.

In the FAO, the U.S. Department of Agriculture (USDA), and the EU Commission, there is mounting pressure to reform agricultural practices to make them more compatible with environmental considerations. The high degree of farmland erosion and soil degradation across the world combined with a better understanding of soil ecosystems has led to a growing acceptance of, for example, conservation agriculture (CA). CA is characterized by zero or minimum tillage, an organic soil cover (a growing crop or a dead mulch left on the surface), direct seeding, and crop rotation.

In CA, seeds are drilled directly into the soil using a zero tillage planter. The surface mulch encourages water and heat retention, as well as the development of soil **biota** that carry out the tillage function naturally, enriching the soil and transferring nutrients to growing plants. With its surface permanently covered, the soil is protected from erosion and can regain its natural balance and fertility. CA embraces the use of pesticides and fertilizers, where necessary, to help maximize its benefits. Once CA is established, the need for chemical additives should be greatly reduced.

According to the FAO, conservation agriculture was being used on about 111 million acres (45 million h) in 2000. The United States was the biggest user at 49 million acres (20 million h). Particularly encouraging has been the rapid spread of CA in Latin America, with Brazil and Argentina leading the way. Its advantages have also been recognized by farmers in Australia and Canada. Elsewhere, the interest has been slower, but the formation of the European Conservation Agricultural Federation in 1999 shows that the idea is spreading. Outside the EU and the United States, the greatest potential for CA is in Africa and Central Asia.

The African Conservation Tillage network (ACT), a Germany-based collection of agricultural experts, is promoting the use of CA on the African continent, where soil degradation and unsustainable farming methods are particularly severe problems. The network was launched following a 1998 workshop on conservation tillage held in Harare by Germany's GTZ (a government-backed development agency), along with the FAO and regional agricultural bodies such as Farm-level Applied Research Methods Programme for East and Southern Africa (FARMESA). As a GTZ press release pointed out, "soil is being degraded and its productivity diminished at an alarming rate in many parts of Africa. Very few land users have adopted techniques for the conservation of soil resources, and in many cases those currently advocated are not appropriate to the soil types, climatic conditions or farming systems."

■■■■ Crop rotation can help farmers prevent soil erosion and reduce their reliance on chemical fertilizers. Some crops, such as corn, use large amounts of nitrogen from the soil. By rotating corn with crops such as alfalfa, which reintroduces nitrogen, the soil has time to recover.

KEY CONCEPTS

Crop rotation Crop rotation involves alternating the types of crops that grow in a certain area every year. This technique has been used for thousands of years. To benefit from rotation, the plants chosen to immediately succeed each other should not make the same demands on the soil (nutrient wise), they should not be susceptible to the same diseases or pests, and they should be of different families. This will also help avoid continuing pest and disease problems. Usually, as part of the rotation, legumes (pod, bean, or pea) are grown to provide available nitrogen for the crops that follow. If crop rotation is done properly, farmers can keep their fields under continuous production, without a need to let them lie fallow or to apply artificial fertilizers, both of which can be expensive.

Ecological balance Ecological balance is a concept that describes a community of organisms as being in a state of equilibrium or balance, in which disturbing one element disturbs the entire system. In most cases, a variety of elements influence the abundance of a species, including predators, food availability, competition with other species, disease, and even the climate. These factors are not constant, but ever-changing. The balance achieved is dynamic, not static. The balance is continually upset by natural events. Ecologists question the existence of an ecological balance because the natural state of any system is not necessarily the preferred state.

Natural competition Natural competition acknowledges a natural rule that within limited living conditions, there is fierce natural competition amongst living beings.

Duties: Designs agricultural equipment and structures; develops ways to conserve soil and water and to improve the processing of agricultural products

Education: Bachelor or master of engineering degree in biological or agricultural science

Interests: Engineering, creative design, environmental protection, agriculture, and mathematics

For further information on agricultural engineering, navigate to **www.bls.gov/oco/ocos261.htm** or go to **www.agriculture.purdue.edu/usda/careers/agengineer.html**

Careers in Focus

Agricultural engineers solve agricultural problems, such as erosion and soil depletion using biological science, engineering principles, and design skills. They work around the world and are involved in all aspects of the production, design, and implementation of soil- and water-conserving machinery, products, and procedures. Agricultural engineers need solid scientific knowledge and superior math skills to be able to perform engineering calculations accurately. They must also be creative in order to develop innovative solutions to environmental problems.

There are many career opportunities for agricultural engineers. Many are consultants to farmers and the farming industry. They make recommendations on the most efficient methods of farming to conserve soil and other environmental resources. Some agricultural engineers work in the equipment industry designing new types of agricultural equipment to improve the environmental impact of the machinery. Other agricultural engineers plan, supervise, and manage the construction of irrigation, drainage, flood, and water control systems in order to conserve soil quality. Some agricultural engineers work in sales or management for farm equipment companies and environmental organizations. Agricultural engineers also can work with governments to make recommendations for new programs and regulations to limit the environmental impact of farming while improving farm production.

Protecting the Soil

Awareness of green issues should include much greater concern for soil quality. There is a need for more careful day-to-day **husbandry** and a longer-term view. For example, the costs of soil erosion and contamination should be taken into account when comparing different approaches to agricultural production and their relative profitability.

Government subsidies (estimated at $350 billion a year worldwide) distort real costs and sometimes encourage farmers to be inefficient as well as to pollute the environment. Moreover, farmers are usually exempted from the principle of "the polluter pays." There may be little incentive to cut down on the use of chemical fertilizers or pesticides or to control potentially harmful runoff into water systems.

Governments in developed countries are beginning to introduce policies to shift agriculture toward more sustainable methods. Though the Bush administration bucked the trend by proposing large additional subsidies to U.S. farmers in 2002, the general direction of policy is to reduce subsidies, penalize polluters, and provide incentives for conservation of ecosystems. There is now a much better understanding of soil degradation, what causes it, and how it can be prevented. The difficulty is to persuade farmers accustomed to industrial methods that alternatives are not only necessary, but in the long term will be just as profitable.

Preventing further soil damage in developing countries will be difficult. Instead of a highly regulated agricultural

---

Soil degradation is often a symptom of poverty—and both problems need to be addressed.

---

industry and a relatively small number of large farms, there are often few regulatory controls and many millions of farmers tending small plots and struggling to feed their families. Many of these farmers have traditionally used mixed farming and pollution-free methods. Over time, they have been persuaded to use chemical fertilizers and pesticides and to grow specialist cash crops in the interest of greater economic efficiency. Untrained in new agricultural technology and too poor to afford the right equipment, many farmers in the developing world misuse fertilizers and pesticides. Short-term survival may take precedence over long-term conservation. Soil degradation is often a symptom of poverty —and both problems need to be addressed.

Climate change provides another reason for concern over soil degradation. Soil organisms play an important part in the carbon and nitrogen cycles. Soil carbon in biota and plant roots is relatively stable but is released into the atmosphere by tillage. Soil carbon losses have been heavy since large-scale agriculture began. The result has been both a reduction in soil fertility and an increase in greenhouse gases. Reversing these two trends is vital to the future health of the planet.

More than 17 million acres (7 million h) of productive land is eroded every year.

The Kyoto Protocol has stimulated much debate about the role of agriculture in climate change. The contribution of global farming to greenhouse gas emissions is estimated at 21–25 percent for carbon dioxide and 55–60 percent for both methane and nitrous oxides. The former results mainly are from the growth of livestock populations and the expansion of wetland rice cultivation; the latter are from the huge amounts of nitrogen applied to the soil as fertilizer over the past 50 years. Since plowed land has reduced **albedo** (it absorbs more heat), the global spread of "brownfield" cropland may also have contributed to global warming.

There is much talk of biofuels being a method that could be used in the future, for example, planting woody crops that can act as carbon reservoirs and then be harvested for renewable fuel. Indeed any trees, crops, or grasses soak up carbon dioxide. According to the Intergovernmental Panel on Climate Change (IPCC), the potential for carbon separation in tropical ecosystems by the year 2010 is 125 megatons (113 Mt) of carbon a year for croplands, 170 megatons (154 Mt) for forests, and 240 megatons (218 Mt) for grazing lands. Interest has been stimulated by the idea of carbon

The Kyoto Protocol has stimulated much debate about the role of agriculture in climate change.

trading, with some countries able to sell their carbon separation "surpluses" to countries with carbon deficits.

The benefits of increasing soil carbon are well documented, as the U.S. Center for Rural Affairs has pointed out. "They include increasing soil fertility, improving the moisture-retaining capacity of the soil, improving nitrogen fertilizer use by crops, and making the soil more resilient to climatic stresses… Unlike trees, grass places proportionally more of the carbon into its roots than into the aboveground

INTERNATIONAL CONVENTIONS THAT HELP TO PROTECT THE LAND

UN Convention on Biological Diversity (CBD) (adopted in 1992, implemented in 1993, ratified by 186 states [but not the United States] by April 2006) The three goals of the CBD are to promote the conservation of biodiversity, the sustainable use of its components, and the fair and equitable sharing of benefits arising out of the utilization of genetic resources. The FAO was given the job of coordinating international efforts to preserve soil biodiversity.

UN Convention to Combat Desertification (adopted in 1994, implemented after 50th ratification in 1996) The convention stresses the need for coordinated action and the full involvement of local people in measures to combat desertification and drought (which affects 70 percent of the world's agricultural drylands and 30 percent of Earth's land area). The convention is being implemented through national action programs, with Africa the top priority.

Stockholm Convention on Persistent Organic Pollutants (adopted in 2001, implemented on may 17, 2004) The convention seeks to eliminate production and use of aldrin, chlordane, dieldrin, endrin, heptachlor, hexachlorobenzene, mirex, toxaphene, polychlorinated biphenyls (PCBs), and dichloro-diphenyl-trichloroethane (DDT) (though some exemptions are permitted). There are also measures to eliminate or reduce unintentional releases of dioxins and furans.

Basel Convention on the Control of Transboundary Movements of Hazardous Waste and their Disposal (adopted 1989, implemented in 1992) The convention seeks to reduce exports of hazardous wastes from developed to developing countries. (An amendment to ban exports awaits ratification.) Separate regional agreements protect the South Pacific region, Africa, and Central America from imports of hazardous waste.

Rotterdam Convention on the Prior Informed Consent Procedure for Certain Hazardous Chemicals and Pesticides in International Trade (adopted 1998, implemented on February 24, 2004) The convention introduces mandatory requirements for information sharing regarding imports and exports of hazardous chemicals.

stem of the plant. Once in the roots, carbon is relatively immobilized, and its pathway to the atmosphere is long and involved."

"We want to emphasize that the national interest here is in building quality soils in which carbon is not merely stashed, but in which it is stabilized as humus by living soil organisms that are part of a healthy, productive cycle of life. This process not only alters carbon from a relatively volatile condition in which it might be readily oxidized back into the atmosphere, but it strengthens its role as an agent of healthy plant production. Soil must be more than just a carbon dump."

Though such views are gaining ground, soil health is not at the top of the political agenda. If food production is to keep up with population growth, soil conservation needs to get the attention of policy makers in national governments around the world.

Fertile soil is able to sustain healthy plant growth.

AGRICULTURAL LAND

Some ancient civilizations had good soil that was ruined by overuse. Examples range from Mesopotamia to North Africa (once the bread basket of the Roman Empire). Mesopotamia, an area of the middle east located between the Tigris and Euphrates rivers and also known as the Fertile Crescent, was inhabited by various civilizations between about 10,000 and 5,000 BC. In both cases, the land that was the inhabitants' primary source of grain was farmed until all nutrients were depleted from it.

The Green Revolution is the name given to a vast increase in food production in the 1960s due to the breeding of new plant varieties and the application of modern agricultural techniques in new areas. Its higher yields are estimated to have helped save more than 988 million acres (400 million h) of land from being turned into farmland.

Two-thirds of potential agricultural land in the developing world is affected by poor natural fertility, poor drainage, sandy or stony soils, or steep slopes. Low or irregular rainfall is also common. On land such as this, soil productivity can only be improved by a combination of new technology and good management. What is needed is an integrated approach, embracing, for example, local knowledge, conservation of water resources, ecofriendly pest control, efficient fertilizer application, crop rotation, and market forces that encourage farmers to apply sustainable methods.

KEY CONCEPTS

Greenhouse gases The six main greenhouse gases are carbon dioxide, hydroflurocarbons, nitrous oxide, sulfur haxafluoride, methane, and perfluorocarbons. Energy radiated by the Sun travels to Earth and warms the surface. Some of the energy becomes trapped in the atmosphere by gases such as carbon dioxide. As a result, the lower portion of Earth's atmosphere experiences a rise in temperature. This is referred to as the "greenhouse effect." Most scientists acknowledge the greenhouse effect, but there is much debate about the causes and effects.

The Kyoto Protocol This international agreement was formally adopted by 84 countries in Kyoto, Japan, in 1997. It requires industrialized countries to reduce their greenhouse gas emissions by 2012. The agreement came into effect in 2005, following ratification by Russia in 2004. As of April 2006, a total of 163 countries have ratified the agreement. Notable exceptions include the United States and Australia. Other countries, such as India and China, which have ratified the protocol, are not required to reduce carbon emissions under the present agreement.

Careers in Focus

There is an economic dimension to most environmental issues. Environmental economists analyze the value of natural resources in relation to their environmental value, as well as their financial value. Their conclusions show the true value of resources both environmentally and economically. These results help governments and organizations decide if environmental policies will have a net benefit in terms of cost, revenue, jobs, public health, and environmental protection.

Today, economics considers social and environmental concerns, as well as traditional dollar issues. Natural resource economists study natural resources and determine the best practices for sustainable use. They consider the proposed usage of land, water, air, and other resources.

Environmental economists use their research skills to examine statistics and advanced computer models. They must have good communication skills as they meet with all kinds of stakeholders, including governments, the public, environmental organizations, industry, and scientists. They also conduct social, economic, and environmental research to assess the benefits and drawbacks of new projects and policies at the local, global, and national level.

The welfare of many people depends on both economic development and environmental conservation. Environmental economists make it their job to present the scientific case for the value of sustainable development.

Timeline of Events

1500 B.C.
Soil erosion is both a consequence of growth and a cause of collapse in Central American city-states.

500 B.C.
Greek coastal cities become landlocked after deforestation, which causes soil erosion. The siltation fills in the bays and mouths of rivers.

A.D. 1748
Jared Eliot writes a series of six essays, *Essays Upon Field Husbandry*, about reducing inefficiency and waste in colonial American farming methods.

1862
The United States Department of Agriculture (USDA) is created.

1928
Soil erosion is identified as a serious threat to agricultural productivity in the United States.

1928
The United States Congress provides funds to the United States Department of Agriculture for soil erosion research.

1931
Severe drought hits the midwestern and southern plains of the United States. As crops die, "black blizzards" begin. Dust from the overplowed and overgrazed land begins to blow.

1932
The number of dust storms increases in the United States to fourteen this year.

1933
The Soil Erosion Service is established in the United States, under the Department of Interior.

1933
Thirty-eight dust storms are reported in the United States.

1934, May
Large dust storms spread from the dust bowl area. The United States experiences its worst drought in history. The drought covers 75 percent of the country and severely affects 27 states.

1934, December
In the United States, about 35 million acres (14 million h) of cultivated land are destroyed for crop production. All or most of the topsoil in 100 million acres (40 million h) of crops is lost. Another are 125 million acres (51 million h) of land rapidly losing topsoil.

1935
The U.S. Congress declares soil erosion "a national menace." The Soil Conservation Service is established. Today, this is the Natural Resources Conservation Service.

1939 forward
Rain finally falls in the midwestern and southern plains of the United States, bringing an end to the drought.

1945
The United Nations forms the Food and Agriculture Organization.

1945–1990
A study by the United Nations, called the Global Assessment of Soil Degradation (GLASOD), estimates that 38 percent of the world's cropland is degraded (74 percent in Central America).

■■■■ **Improper disposal of industrial wastes can lead to toxic contamination of soil and water.**

1970
The United States Environmental Protection Agency (EPA) is established to protect human health and to safeguard the natural environment.

1977
The United States Congress passes the Soil and Water Conservation Act.

1978
The president of the United States declares an emergency at Love Canal, a chemical waste disposal site in Niagara Falls turned residential area whose contents leaked due to container damage, causing extremely high rates cancer and birth defects for the neighborhood.

1997
The Kyoto Protocol is adopted by the United States and 84 other nations, but it is not ratified by the United States Congress.

2002
The European Forum on Agricultural Research for Development (EFARD) reports that two-thirds of agricultural land has been affected by soil degradation over the past 50 years.

2002
China increases per capita cereal production by 48 percent since 1970. It falls by 9 percent in Africa.

2002
Six percent of the population of the Organization for Economic Cooperation and Development (OECD) countries is employed in agriculture.

2002
Forest cover in the developing world falls by 800,000 square miles (2 million sq km) since 1980.

2004
Stockholm Convention on Persistent Organic Pollutants enters into force in May. Convention members seek to eliminate production and use of aldrin, chlordane, dieldrin, endrin, heptachlor, hexachlorobenzene, mirex, toxaphene, PCBs, and DDT.

2005
The Kyoto Protocol comes into effect, without the support of the United States and Australia.

2006
The world population reaches 6.5 billion according to the U.S. Census Bureau.

2025 (projected)
Sub-Saharan Africa will only be able to feed 40 percent of its expected one billion person population

Concept Web

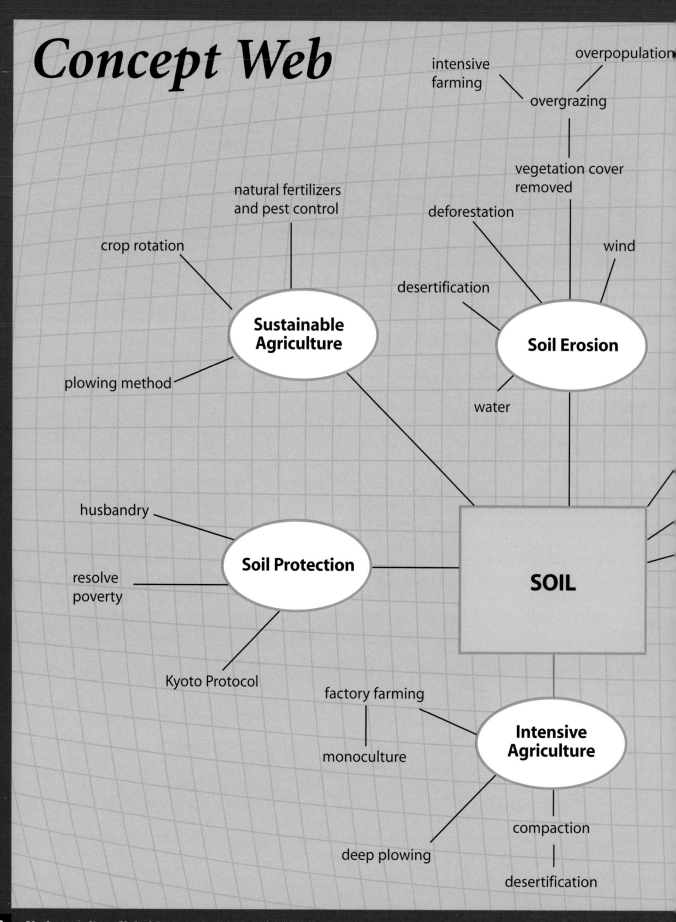

intensive farming

overpopulation

overgrazing

vegetation cover removed

deforestation

wind

natural fertilizers and pest control

crop rotation

desertification

Sustainable Agriculture

Soil Erosion

plowing method

water

husbandry

Soil Protection

SOIL

resolve poverty

Kyoto Protocol

factory farming

Intensive Agriculture

monoculture

compaction

deep plowing

desertification

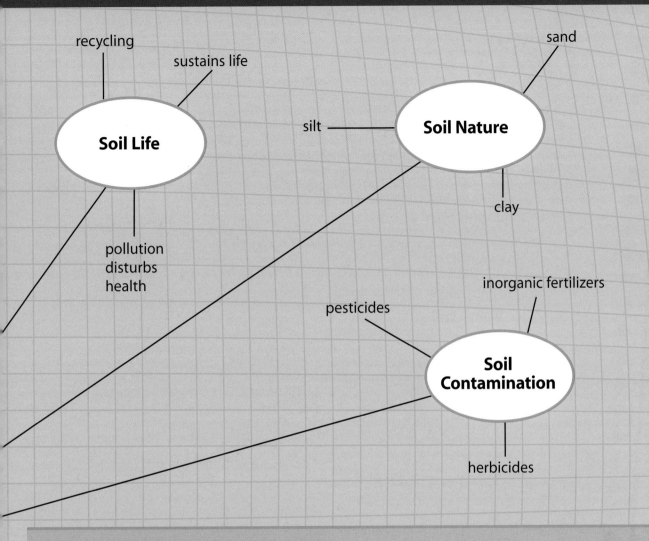

recycling

sustains life

sand

Soil Life

silt —— **Soil Nature**

clay

pollution
disturbs
health

inorganic fertilizers

pesticides

Soil Contamination

herbicides

MAKE YOUR OWN CONCEPT WEB

A concept web is a useful summary tool. It can also be used to plan your research or help you write an essay or report. To make your own concept web, follow the steps below:

- You will need a large piece of unlined paper and a pencil.
- First, read through your source material, such as *Land Abuse and Soil Erosion* in the Understanding Global Issues series.
- Write the main idea, or concept, in large letters in the center of the page.
- On a sheet of lined paper, jot down all words, phrases, or lists that you know are connected with the concept. Try to do this from memory.
- Look at your list. Can you group your words and phrases in certain topics or themes? Connect the different topics with lines to the center, or to other "branches."
- Critique your concept web. Ask questions about the material on your concept web: Does it all make sense? Are all the links shown? Could there be other ways of looking at it? Is anything missing?
- What more do you need to find out? Develop questions for those areas you are still unsure about or where information is missing. Use these questions as a basis for further research.

Quiz

Multiple Choice

1. What are some of the key negative costs incurred in factory farming?
   a) keeping a veterinarian on duty to maintain the health of the animals
   b) feeding the animals for a long time
   c) soil degradation and environmental costs
   d) all of the above

2. How long does it take to create a layer of soil sufficient to support agriculture?
   a) 10 years
   b) 3,000–12,000 years
   c) 1,000 years
   d) 1 year

3. What do earthworms and termites do that benefits the soil?
   a) they eat other insects, making less debris in the soil
   b) they aerate the soil, thus maintaining its fertility
   c) they make room for plants to grow
   d) all of the above

4. What is the key concern about using slash and burn techniques?
   a) runoff easily occurs
   b) any plants remaining burn easily
   c) weeds grow in abundance
   d) desert areas are produced

5. How much of the total land area in Europe is threatened with erosion?
   a) 16 percent
   b) 25 percent
   c) 50 percent
   d) 83 percent

6. What are some of the concerns involved with using pesticides?
   a) eventually, pests become immune to them
   b) the chemicals end up in food and water
   c) plants are killed along with insects
   d) all of the above

7. What can be done to ensure sustainable agriculture?
   a) genetic engineering and hydroponics
   b) intensive farming
   c) continuous cropping
   d) crop rotation and natural methods of fertilization and pest control

Where Did It Happen?

1. Livestock numbers have grown rapidly, putting extra pressure on land resources.
2. The government proposed large additional subsidies to farmers.
3. This country has become a net importer of wheat because their farmers can no longer produce enough good quality wheat to meet domestic demand.
4. Livestock farming has greatly exacerbated the problem of desertification.

True or False

1. Techniques, such as contour cultivation, grass hedging, and tree planting, can reduce erosion by 50 percent.
2. Acid rain has doubled even though there have been controls on fossil fuel emissions since the 1980s.
3. Many landfill sites are not properly sealed and contamination can eventually reach into groundwater systems.
4. Contaminated soil carries its toxicity into the sea where it can damage aquatic plants and animals.

Answers on page 53

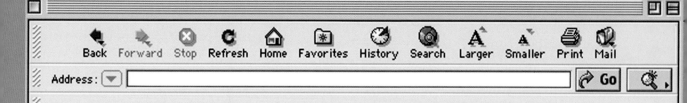

Internet Resources

The following websites provide information about soil loss and erosion:

International Soil and Reference Information Center (ISRIC)
www.isric.nl
The ISRIC aims to provide a better understanding of soils and to promote the sustainable use of land. As the world data center for soil, ISRIC provides the intentional scientific community with accurate and organized soil information. It also works to educate the public about issues surrounding soil quality and sustainable agriculture.

Food and Agriculture Organization of the United Nations (FAO)
www.fao.org
The FAO works to increase world food production by increasing soil productivity throughout the world. They encourage the use of responsible farming techniques including erosion management, effective fertilizer use, and contamination prevention.

World Resources Institute (WRI)
www.wri.org
The WRI is an independent nongovernmental organization founded 20 years ago. Its mission includes the sustainable use of Earth's natural resources. The WRI works to reverse depletion of biological resources while providing people with the food and goods they need to encourage sustainable enterprise, including agricultural production. They also provide public access to information and governmental decisions about natural resources and environmental issues.

Some websites stay current longer than others. To find other soil erosion websites, enter terms such as "soil erosion" and "soil loss" into a search engine.

Further Reading

Food and Agriculture Organization of the United Nations Publications
  - 2000: *Land Resource Potential and Constraints at Regional and Country Levels*
  - 2000: *Manual on Integrated Soil Management and Conservation Practices*
  - 2001: *Soil Carbon Sequestration for Improved Land Management*
  - 2002: *World Reference Base for Soil Resources*
  - 2003: *Biological Management of Soil Ecosystems for Sustainable Agriculture*
  - 2003: *Land and Agriculture* (from United Nations Conference on Environment and Development (UNCED), Rio de Janeiro 1992 to World Summit on Sustainable Development 2002)
  - 2003: *Organic Agriculture, Environment, and Food Security*
  - 2003: *Unlocking the Water Potential of Agriculture*

Gobat, Jean-Michel, Michel Aragno, and Willy Matthey. *The Living Soil: Fundamentals of Soil Science and Soil Biology.* Enfield, N.H.: Science Publishers Inc., 2004.

Hellin, Jon. *Better Land Husbandry: An International Guide to Effective Practices.* Enfield, N.H.: Science Publishers Inc., 2004.

Richter, Daniel D. et al. *Understanding Soil Change: Soil Sustainability over Millennia, Centuries, and Decades.* Cambridge: Cambridge University Press, 2001.

Toy, Terrence J. et al. Soil Erosion: *Processes, Prediction, Measurement, and Control.* New York: John Wiley & Sons. 3rd edition, 2002.

Answers

Multiple Choice
  1. c) 2. b) 3. b) 4. d) 5. a) 6. b) 7. d)

Where Did It Happen?
  1. China 2. United States 3. Denmark 4. Australia

True or False
  1. T 2. F 3. T 4. T

Glossary

acidification: the process of becoming acid or being converted into an acid

adsorption: the taking up of a gas or liquid by the surface of a solid; it involves molecular attraction at the surface

albedo: the ratio of light reflected from a surface to the amount that strikes it

bioengineering: brings together physical, chemical, or mathematical sciences and engineering methods and techniques for the study of biology, medicine, behavior, or health

biota: the plant and animal life of a region

contaminated: polluted with harmful materials

degradation: the state or condition of a species or group that changes to a lower state

desertification: deterioration of arid land into desert, caused by a change in climate or by overuse by people and/or animals

erosion: the removal of the top layer of soil by natural forces, such as water, glaciers, or wind

guano: droppings of birds or bats

humus: organic soil material formed by the decay of animal or vegetable matter

husbandry: the practice of cultivating the land or raising stock; conservative management

Industrial Revolution: the change from an agricultural to an industrial society, which began in England in the mid-18th century and is continuing in some countries today

organic farming: farming without the use of synthetic fertilizers, pesticides, and drugs

overgrazing: the damage to vegetation when too many animals over consume an area

regolith: the layer of rocky debris and dust covering the bedrock surface of planets, satellites, and asteroids, comprising soil, sand, rock fragments, volcanic ash, and glacial drift

rill: a small drainage channel cut in a slope by the flow of water, which can become wider and deeper with continuing erosion

root respiration: the consumption of oxygen and the release of carbon dioxide and water in roots

salinization: the process of becoming overly salty

sheet: any broad thin expanse or surface; initial surface erosion by water running off as sheets

subsidies: financial aid given by the government to an individual, company, or another government

sustainable: a method of harvesting or using a resource so that it is not depleted or permanently damaged

sustainable agriculture: method of farming that attempts to minimize damage to the environment

topsoil: the fertile upper layer of soil

toxic: a poisonous and hazardous substance

Index

Credits

All of the Internet URLs given in the book were valid at the time of publication. However, due to the dynamic nature of the Internet, some addresses may have changed, or sites may have ceased to exist since publication. While the author and publisher regret any inconvenience this may cause readers, no responsibility for any such changes can be accepted by either the author or the publisher.

Every reasonable effort has been made to trace ownership and to obtain permission to reprint copyright material. The publishers would be pleased to have any errors or omissions brought to their attention so that they may be corrected in subsequent printings.